30 HERBAL GIFTS

Enchanting gift ideas with fresh and dried herbs

LORENZ BOOKS

This edition published by Lorenz Books
an imprint of
Anness Publishing Limited
Hermes House
88-89 Blackfriars Road
London SE1 8HA

Published in the USA by Lorenz Books
Anness Publishing Inc., 27 West 20th Street, New York, NY 10011;
(800) 354-9657

This edition distributed in Canada by Raincoast Books
8680 Cambie Street, Vancouver, British Columbia V6P 6M9

A CIP catalogue record for this book is available from the British Library

ISBN 0-75480-695-2

Publisher: Joanna Lorenz
Project Editor: Fiona Eaton
Designer: Lilian Lindblom
Illustrations: Anna Koska

Printed and bound in Singapore

1 3 5 7 9 10 8 6 4 2

Contents

INTRODUCTION

Making a gift for someone shows that you really are thinking about them, and if you are able to use herbs and flowers grown in your own garden as well, the gift will be doubly appreciated, and particularly pleasurable for you to create. This book is packed with ideas to inspire you. There are original creations using fresh herbs, lovely, long-lasting decorations scented with dried leaves and flowers, and fragrant indulgences for the bath. You will find gifts for all occasions: from a tiny nosegay to majestic topiary trees for a formal interior.

The usefulness, beauty and fragrance of herbs is once more fully appreciated these days. Their lovely natural perfumes are unfailingly popular and all these pretty things take full advantage of their scent as well as their visual appeal. Don't be afraid to include culinary herbs in decorative pieces – in fact, it's a joy to be able to pluck a sprig of rosemary from a beautiful wreath on the wall, rather than taking it from a jar in the cupboard. Although most herbs are grown for their leaves rather than their flowers, these too can be attractive, and if you grow mint or marjoram, for instance, you'll be able to include their flowers in fresh arrangements.

Lavender makes a wonderful ingredient for herbal gifts, whether fresh or dried. Everyone loves its beautiful scent, and while its rich deep blue is a perfect foil for summer roses, it also looks effective in dried winter arrangements, framing creamy candles or combined with russet cinnamon sticks. The best time to pick stems of lavender for drying is just as the flowers are opening and after the morning dew has disappeared.

Tradition has not been overlooked among these projects: you will find instructions for making pomanders and lavender bags, together with some old-fashioned recipes for skin and hair care, alongside the many original suggestions.

ROSE AND FENNEL BOUQUET

A simple but striking combination of yellow roses, lime-green fennel and delicate birch leaves is complemented by a natural raffia bow. This hand-tied bouquet is easy to assemble: just keep turning the arrangement as you add the stems in a spiral shape.

MATERIALS

20 stems yellow roses
5 stems fennel
15 stems birch leaves
twine
scissors
raffia

1 Strip all but the top 15 cm (6 in) of the yellow rose stems clean of leaves and thorns. Split the multi-headed stems of fennel, so that each stem has only one head. Strip all but the top 15 cm (6 in) of the birch stems clean of leaves.

2 Hold one rose in the hand and add individual stems of fennel, birch and rose in a continuing sequence, all the while turning the bunch so that the stems form a spiral shape. Continue until all the stems are used.

3 Tie the bouquet with twine at the point where the stems cross. Cut the bottom of the stems so that they measure about one-third of the overall height of the finished bouquet.

4 Complete the bouquet by tying raffia over the twine and finishing with a bow. Trim the ends of the raffia.

FRAGRANT NOSEGAY

This tiny herbal posy (nosegay) is made up of tight concentric circles of herbs around a central flower, and it will exude a marvellous mixture of scents. Nosegays were popular in Elizabethan times for warding off unpleasant smells when walking in the street.

MATERIALS

scissors
1 chive flower
flowering mint
rosemary
fennel
lemon geranium leaves
twine
raffia

1 Cut all the plant stems to a length suitable for your posy (nosegay) and clean them of leaves and thorns. Holding the chive flower and flowering mint in your hand, add stems of rosemary and fennel, turning the bunch as you work. Complete a circle with each type of herb before you change to another. For the final circle, use lemon geranium leaves to edge the bunch.

TIP
Nosegays made with herbs can be used for culinary as well as decorative purposes. Alternatively, they can be left to dry, to provide lasting pleasure.

2 When everything is in position, tie the bunch with twine and trim the stem ends neatly so that they are all the same length. Complete the nosegay by tying raffia over the twine and finishing with a bow.

SCENTED LEAF NAPKIN TIE

This beautiful alternative to a napkin ring is easy to make and very effective in enhancing the look of a dinner table. The method is simply to use any reasonably sturdy trailing foliage to bind the napkin and then to create a focal point by adding leaves, berries or flower heads of your choice. You can adapt this idea to many different occasions by using different types of flowers and herbs.

MATERIALS

long, thin, flexible stem rosemary
napkin
3 lemon geranium leaves
2 or 3 heads flowering mint
scissors

1 Find a suitable stem of rosemary, long and flexible enough to wrap around the rolled napkin once or twice. Tie the stem securely.

2 Arrange the lemon geranium leaves and the heads of flowering mint by gently pushing their stems through the knot of the binding rosemary stem. Trim any excess stems.

TIP
If you feel you need to fix the herbs more firmly, wire the leaves and flower heads before attaching them to the binding material.

FRESH HERBAL WREATH

In many parts of Europe it is believed that a herb wreath hung in a kitchen, or by the entrance of a house, is a sign of welcome, wealth and good luck. This wreath will stay fresh for 2–3 weeks because the stems of the herbs are in water, but even when it dries out it will continue to look good for some time.

MATERIALS

30 cm (12 in) diameter florist's foam wreath frame
2 branches bay leaves
2 bunches rosemary
6 large garlic bulbs (heads)
6 or 7 beetroot (beets)
stub (floral) wires
scissors
40 stems flowering marjoram
40 stems flowering mint

TIP

As well as being a decorative feature, a herb wreath can also be useful in the kitchen. The herbs can be taken from it and used for cooking without causing too much damage to the overall design.

1 Soak the florist's foam wreath frame thoroughly in cold water. Create the background by making a foliage outline using evenly distributed bay leaves and sprigs of rosemary. To ensure an even covering of greenery, position the leaves on the inside, on the top and on the outside of the wreath frame.

2 Wire the garlic bulbs (heads) and beetroot (beets) by pushing two stub (floral) wires through their bases so that they cross. Then pull the projecting wires down and cut to the correct length for the depth of the foam. Decide where on the wreath they are to be positioned and push the wires firmly into the foam.

3 Use the remaining herbs to fill in the spaces in the wreath, concentrating the flowering marjoram around the beetroot (beets) and the flowering mint around the garlic.

LAVENDER TUSSIE MUSSIE

In bygone days, ladies carried herbal tussie mussies, or posies (mini-bouquets), as a personal perfume. Nowadays, tussie mussies make a pretty gift. The scent of fresh lavender is particularly soothing and a bunch will dry beautifully. White lavender contrasted with the more conventional blue lavender makes a startling tussie mussie.

MATERIALS

1 bunch deep blue lavender
1 bunch white lavender
green raffia, twine or elastic band
secateurs (pruners)
wide ribbon

1 Arrange a circle of deep blue lavender stems around the stems of a small bunch of white lavender. Secure with a piece of green raffia, twine or an elastic band.

2 Arrange the remaining white lavender around the blue lavender and secure the bunch with more raffia, twine or an elastic band. Trim the stalks to an even length.

3 Complete the arrangement by tying a length of wide ribbon around the posy (bouquet) to cover the green raffia, twine or elastic binding. Tie the ribbon in a bow.

MIXED HERB CANDLE RING

This pretty little candle ring is created on a very small plastic foam ring. Place the floral ring over the candlestick to create a simple but effective decoration. Filled with a heady combination of fennel, rosemary, lemon geranium, hyssop and violas, it is the perfect decoration to create an intimate dinner table.

MATERIALS

*15 cm (6 in) diameter florist's foam
wreath frame
candlestick
scissors
rosemary
lemon geranium leaves
fennel
hyssop
violas*

1 Soak the florist's foam wreath frame thoroughly in cold water. Set it in place around the candlestick and start to add the plant material. Cut the plant stems to an even length. Make a basic outline with stems of rosemary and lemon geranium leaves. Position them evenly around and all over the ring, to produce a full effect.

TIP
Never leave the candle burning unattended, and do not allow it to burn down to less than 5 cm (2 in) from the foliage.

2 Arrange the fennel and hyssop evenly between the rosemary and lemon geranium leaves, filling in any gaps. Finally, tuck in a few viola flowers around the wreath to add splashes of colour.

FRESH LAVENDER HEART

There really is nothing quite so romantic as a heart made entirely of fresh lavender. Make one for a special occasion, then let it dry naturally as an everlasting souvenir. The materials used in this example make a heart measuring about 30 cm (12 in) across.

MATERIALS

secateurs (pruners) or scissors
120 stems lavender
florist's silver roll wire
garden wire
wire cutters
florist's tape (stem-wrap tape)
green raffia

1 Cut the lavender stems to 2.5 cm (1 in) and make up bunches containing about six heads each. Secure them firmly with florist's silver roll wire.

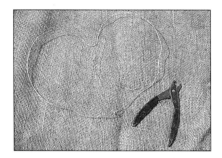

2 Make a hook at each end of a piece of garden wire about 112 cm (44 in) long. Link to make a circle, then make a dip at the top and bend into a heart shape.

3 Using florist's tape (stem-wrap tape), bind the first bunch of lavender to the bottom of the wire heart. Bind the next bunch a little further up the wire and continue until you reach the centre. Work up the other side in the same way.

4 Make a small bunch of lavender and secure with wire. Tie with green raffia. Place at the bottom of the front of the wreath and bend the stalks to the back. Pass the raffia to the back to catch the stems and then secure at the front with a bow.

TIP
This example uses a lot of lavender, so make sure that you have access to plenty before you begin. If you don't have enough, use a smaller wire base.

CANDLELIT HERB RING

*In this original table decoration, a wreath of white dill, softly lit with night-lights
(tea-lights), is set around a group of individual terracotta pots, each containing
a different herb. Use pots of various sizes within the ring to give height and
interest to the arrangement.*

MATERIALS

*30 cm (12 in) diameter florist's foam
wreath frame
2 blocks florist's foam
6 night-lights (tea-lights)
4 terracotta pots
cellophane (plastic wrap)
craft knife
white dill
rosemary
mint
marjoram
guelder-rose (European cranberry)
berries*

TIP

This display can be dismantled and
the parts used separately, to good
effect, in different situations. The
herbs in the individual terracotta
pots can even be dried to extend
their usefulness. Never leave
burning candles unattended.

1 Soak the florist's foam wreath
frame and the blocks of florist's
foam thoroughly in cold water. Press
the night-lights (tea-lights) into the
soaked florist's foam wreath frame,
spacing them equally around its
circumference. Line the terracotta
pots with cellophane (plastic wrap)
to prevent leakage. Using the craft
knife, cut the florist's foam and fit it
firmly into the pots.

2 Push the white dill into the foam
wreath frame between the night-
lights (tea-lights). Then mass the
individual pots with selected herbs
and foliage such as rosemary, mint,
marjoram, guelder-rose (European
cranberry) berries. For the best effect,
fill each pot with one type of herb
only. Place the ring in position and
arrange the pots within it.

ROSE AND FENNEL BUTTONHOLE

Lime-green fennel seed heads contrast in colour and texture with the other vivid elements of this stunning buttonhole: a yellow rose, elaeagnus leaves and orange-red rosehips. The result is a simple, visually strong decoration suitable for either a man or a woman to wear at a summer wedding.

MATERIALS

scissors
1 yellow rose
stub (floral) wires
florist's silver roll wire
5 elaeagnus leaves, graded in size
15 rosehips and leaves
1 head fennel
florist's tape (stem-wrap tape)
pin

1 Cut the rose stem to 4 cm (1½ in) and attach a stub (floral) wire. Use florist's silver roll wire for the other elements. Thread the wire through each of the elaeagnus leaves. Group 4 cm (1½ in) stems of rosehips in bunches of five and wire together. Divide the head of fennel into its component stems and wire in groups. Tape all the wired elements.

2 Keeping the rose head central to the arrangement, bind the bunches of fennel and rosehips around it with silver roll wire. Bind the elaeagnus leaves to the arrangement with silver roll wire, placing the largest leaf at the back of the rose, the two smallest leaves at the front and two medium-sized leaves at the side.

3 Trim the wires to about 7 cm (2¾ in) and tape them with florist's tape (stem-wrap tape). Look closely at the completed buttonhole and, if necessary, bend the leaves down to form a framework for the rose and adjust the overall shape so that the back of the decoration is flat for pinning to a lapel.

TIP
As with all buttonholes, the construction involves wiring the stems, which is time-consuming. Make sure you leave yourself plenty of time to create this arrangement on the day.

FLOWER-EDGED BASKET

This small, flower-trimmed basket is scented with bunches of fragrant lavender and marjoram, and will be a welcome gift on any occasion. A piece of foam inside the basket, with moss packed around it to keep it in place, supports the candle. Choose a pale creamy-white candle for the centre of this arrangement, to set off the subtle, natural tones of the flowers and seed heads.

MATERIALS

florist's silver roll wire
sphagnum moss
round basket
wire cutters
Achillea ptarmica
lavender
marjoram
scissors
stub (floral) wires
poppy seed heads
glue gun
mintola balls
mossing (floral) pins
green moss
florist's dry foam block
candle

1 Wire a "collar" of sphagnum moss around the outer edge of the basket. Separate the flowers and trim the stems to 15 cm (6 in). Create small bunches of each type, wiring them in the centre of the stems. Push them into the moss, one variety at a time, in small groups. Criss-cross the stems so that some flowers face outwards and some inwards.

2 Trim the poppy stems directly under the seed heads, and glue these and the mintola balls in small groups around the basket using the glue gun. Use the poppy seed heads to cover any stub (floral) wires that may be showing on the centre-wired bunches of flowers. Make sure that everything is distributed evenly around the circle.

3 Using the mossing (floral) pins, fix green moss to fill any small gaps. Pay particular attention to any stub (floral) wire and the outer edge of the moss collar. Use the green moss in generous handfuls so that the ring has an even shape. Put the foam block into the basket and stand the candle on top.

MARJORAM AND BAY TREE

Herbs are the main ingredients of this picturesque potted "tree". Oregano will keep its colour for a very long time, so it's ideal for a dried arrangement in a bright location. If you have access to fresh stems of bay, add them straight from the bush and they will slowly dry out.

MATERIALS

terracotta flowerpot
self-hardening clay
38 cm (15 in) branch
reindeer moss
mossing (floral) pins
glue gun
15 cm (6 in) diameter florist's dry foam sphere
8–10 bunches marjoram
stub (floral) wires
wire cutters
pliers
bay stems
knife
oregano
twig bundles

1 Fill the bottom of the terracotta flowerpot with self-hardening clay and set the branch centrally in it. Fix the reindeer moss around the base of the branch, using the mossing (floral) pins. Leave the base to dry and harden completely. If the clay is hard when you fix the moss, use the glue gun rather than the pins. When the base is dry, lift it out and glue it inside the pot. Push the foam sphere on to the top of the branch.

2 Bunch and wire all the marjoram, making sure each bunch is no more than 10 cm (4 in) in length. Push the bunches, one at a time, into the foam sphere, always supporting the opposite side of the foam to ensure that you do not push the sphere off the top of the branch. Remember to stand back from the display as you work, to check that you have added all the bunches evenly and kept the shape of the sphere.

TIP

Keep all the bunches as even as possible, and the same length. This helps when putting the tree together, and will ensure that you achieve a perfect sphere. When the display has started to look a little tired, it can be sprayed with florist's clear lacquer to bring back some of the colour.

3 Continue to add bunches of marjoram until the whole of the foam sphere has been covered. Cut the bay stems vertically to separate sprays of one or two leaves. Wire them in bunches or individually. Wire the oregano.

4 Turn the whole tree upside-down and push the bay stems and oregano into the foam, all around the top of the branch. There should be no bay stems showing. Finally, wire the bundles of twigs and attach to the arrangement.

CLOVE AND ORANGE POMANDERS

The traditional pomander starts as a fresh orange that, as you use it, dries into a beautiful decoration with a warm spicy smell evocative of mulled wine and the festive season. Several pomanders, tied with different ribbons, make a lovely Christmas gift. They can be displayed together in a bowl, hung up around the house, used as Christmas decorations or put in a wardrobe to scent its contents.

MATERIALS

3 contrasting lengths of ribbon
3 small, firm oranges
cloves
scissors

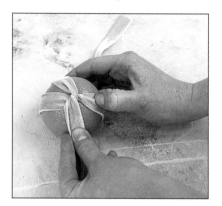

1 Tie a length of ribbon around each orange as if you were tying it around a parcel. Cross it over at the base and bring the ends up to the top of the orange.

2 Finish off by tying the ribbon in a bow. Adjust the position of the ribbon as necessary to ensure that the orange is divided into four equal-sized sections.

TIP
The oranges will shrink as they dry out, so you will probably need to tighten the ribbons and re-tie the bows.

3 Starting at the edges of the sections, push the sharp ends of the cloves into the exposed orange skin and continue until each quarter is completely covered. Trim the ends of the ribbon neatly.

CINNAMON ADVENT CANDLE

This advent candle marks the countdown to Christmas in a novel way: with a spiral of 25 cinnamon sticks of decreasing height. Each day the candle is lit to burn down to the top of the next cinnamon stick until, finally, on Christmas Day it is level with the shortest. As a bonus, the heat of the flame releases the spicy aroma of the cinnamon.

MATERIALS

25 medium thickness cinnamon sticks
1 candle, 7.5 x 23 cm (3 x 9 in)
raffia
scissors
10 cm (4 in) diameter florist's foam
wreath frame
stub (floral) wires
reindeer moss
20 dried red roses
all-purpose glue

1 Strap the cinnamon sticks around the candle with the raffia. Pull them down, reducing their height by equal stages, so that they spiral around the candle; the shortest should be about 6 cm (2¼ in) from the base.

2 Bind the cinnamon sticks securely at two points with raffia, and cut the excess lengths of the sticks flush with the base of the candle. Be careful not to splinter the sticks when trimming them.

TIP

Never leave the candle burning unattended, and do not allow it to burn down to less than 5 cm (2 in) from the base of the arrangement.

3 Push the candle into the foam ring. Make hairpin shapes from the stub (floral) wires and pin moss on to the foam to cover the ring.

4 Cut the rose stems to 2.5 cm (1 in) and brush glue on to their bases and stems. Push into the foam through the moss around the candle.

SPICY STAR WALL DECORATION

Make a fragrant rustic star from long cinnamon sticks, embellished with bunches of lavender to add colour and a contrasting texture. The heady scent of lavender mixes well with the warm, spicy cinnamon. Take care when handling the long cinnamon sticks, as they can be brittle.

MATERIALS

15 cinnamon sticks, 30 cm (12 in) long
raffia
scissors
75 stems lavender
ribbon

1 Divide the cinnamon sticks into five groups of three. Interlace the ends of two groups of sticks to form a point and secure firmly with raffia. Trim the ends of the raffia.

2 Continue interlacing and binding together groups of cinnamon sticks to create a star-shaped frame. Bind the sticks together where they cross each other to make the frame rigid.

3 Divide the lavender into five bunches of 15 stems each. Turn the star shape so that the binding knots are at the back. Attach lavender to the front of the frame, using raffia, at the crossing points of the cinnamon sticks.

4 When all the lavender bunches have been secured, make a small bow from the ribbon and tie it to the decoration at the lower crossing point in the middle of the star.

TIP
You can adapt this design to make a Christmas star by substituting dried fruit slices and gilded seed heads for the lavender. You may also prefer to use straight twigs instead of the cinnamon sticks.

ROSEBUD AND CARDAMOM POMANDER

*Rosebud pomanders are fun to make and add a pretty touch to a room,
hanging beneath a shelf or over a dressing-table mirror. The pale green,
exotically scented cardamom pods provide a contrast in texture and
colour, whether you choose yellow, white or pink roses.*

MATERIALS

*ribbon or cord for hanging
stub (floral) wire
7.5 cm (3 in) florist's dry foam ball
scissors
small rosebuds
all-purpose glue
green cardamom pods*

TIP

The colour of the rosebuds will
fade over time, but this adds to
their charm. However, when the
ball has faded too much, it can be
sprayed gold and given a new lease
of life as a Christmas ornament.

1 Make a long loop with the
ribbon or cord. Bind the base of
the loop with a stub (floral) wire.
Leave a long end of wire and push
this right through the centre of the
florist's dry foam ball and out the
other side. Trim the excess wire to
about 2.5 cm (1 in) and bend the end
over to lose it in the foam ball.

2 Trim the stems of the rosebuds
to about 2.5 cm (1 in) and stick
them into the foam ball. Use a little
glue if the stems are very short.
Cover the entire ball with rosebuds,
pressing them close together to
conceal the foam ball. Once the foam
ball is completely covered with rosebuds, glue some cardamom pods in
the spaces between them.

FABRIC-COVERED LAVENDER CANDLE POT

With its rich colour and long-lasting heady perfume, lavender is always welcome. You can even add a few drops of lavender oil to the arrangement to boost the impact of the scent. Trim the pot with raffia to give a slightly rustic feel or, for a smarter look, make a fabric or ribbon bow.

MATERIALS

terracotta flowerpot
fabric
scissors
craft knife
florist's dry foam block
mossing (floral) pins
stub (floral) wires
candle
florist's tape (stem-wrap tape)
glue gun (optional)
lavender
moss
raffia

1 Stand the terracotta flowerpot in the middle of the fabric and cut a circle large enough to cover the sides of the pot with 8 cm (3¼ in) to spare. Tuck the excess fabric into the flowerpot, spacing the folds in the fabric evenly around the sides.

2 Trim the florist's dry foam block to the size of the base of the flowerpot. Make sure that it is a tight fit. Push the trimmed foam firmly into the bottom of the flowerpot so that it holds the fabric in place.

3 Bind mossing (floral) pins or stub (floral) wires to the base of the candle with florist's tape (stem-wrap tape) and push into the foam. Alternatively, glue the candle in place.

4 Wire the lavender in small bunches. Working around the pot, push them into the foam so that they lean well out.

5 Make a complete circle of lavender. Fill the space around the candle with moss. Fix it in place with mossing (floral) pins, keeping it clear of the candle. Finish with a raffia bow.

NATURAL CHRISTMAS DECORATIONS

Raid the store cupboard and scrap box, add garden clippings and dried fruit slices, and you have the ingredients for delightful Christmas decorations that can be individually hung or strung on to twine to make a garland.

MATERIALS

stub (floral) wires
small twigs
picture framer's wax gilt
dried bay leaves
dried pear slices
fabric scraps
dried apple slices
dried orange slices
small elastic bands
cinnamon sticks
gold twine
beeswax candle ends

1 Wire together small bundles of twigs with stub (floral) wires, then gild them by rubbing in picture framer's wax gilt with your finger.

2 Make a loop at one end of a stub (floral) wire. Thread on some dried bay leaves, then a dried pear slice. Make a hook at the top.

3 Tie a scrap of coloured fabric to the bottom loop and a scrap of green at the top, to look like leaves. Make apple-slice bundles by threading thick apple slices and bay leaves on to stub (floral) wire.

4 Wire pairs of thin apple slices by passing a wire through the centre of each and twisting them together at the top. Wire the orange slices in the same way. Use small elastic bands to make bundles of cinnamon sticks.

5 Either hang each decoration on the tree or make a garland to hang on the tree or at the window by stringing the decorations on gold twine. The beeswax candle ends are knotted in at intervals.

SPICE TOPIARY

*Fashion a delightfully aromatic, culinary topiary from cloves and
star anise, put it in a terracotta pot decorated with cinnamon sticks and
top with a cinnamon-stick cross. Sticking all the cloves into the florist's
foam is both easy to do and wonderfully therapeutic.*

MATERIALS

*craft knife
cinnamon sticks
small "long Tom" terracotta
flowerpot
glue gun
1 plastic foam cone for dried flowers,
23 cm (9 in) tall
1 small plastic foam cone
stub (floral) wires
about 20 star anise
cloves*

1 Cut the cinnamon sticks to
the length of the flowerpot and
glue them in position. Trim the top
of the larger plastic foam cone. Cut
the smaller cone to fit inside the pot.

2 Put four stub (floral) wires
upright in the pot so they project
above the foam. Use these wires to
stake the trimmed cone on top of the
foam-filled pot.

TIP
This lovely topiary would make an
ideal house-warming present, or a
thoughtful gift for someone who
loves cooking.

3 Wire the star anise up by passing
a wire over the front in one
direction, and another wire over the
front in another direction so that
they cross each other. Twist the
wires together at the back and trim
to about 1 cm (½ in).

4 Push the star anise into the foam
cone in rows – about three down
each side to quarter the cone. Put
two vertically between each row.
Then fill the remaining area of cone
with cloves, packing them tightly so
none of the foam shows through.

5 Glue two short pieces of
cinnamon stick to form a cross.
Wire this up, and use it to decorate
the top of the topiary.

HERB BATH-BAG

Pamper a busy friend with the ingredients for a traditional herbal bath by filling a fine muslin bag with relaxing herbs. The bag can be tied to the taps so that the hot water runs through it. This drawstring design means that the bag can be re-used time after time if it is filled with fresh herbs. Chamomile and hops are relaxing; basil and sage are invigorating.

MATERIALS

silky muslin, 30 x 40 cm (12 x 16 in)
pins
tape measure
matching sewing thread
needle
scissors
cotton fabric scraps, for casing
1 m (3 ft 3 in) narrow ribbon
safety pin
dried herbs to fill, such as chamomile and hops, or basil and sage

1 With right sides together, fold over 5 cm (2 in) of the silky muslin at both short ends. Pin and stitch each short side seam, leaving a 1 cm (½ in) seam allowance. Trim the seams and turn the ends right-side out. Press flat, then turn in the raw edges of the folded ends, pin and sew a narrow hem.

2 Cut two strips of cotton, 3 cm (1¼ in) wide, to fit across the width of the muslin plus 1 cm (½ in). Turn in and press 5 mm (¼ in) hems around each strip. Hem the ends, then pin to the right side of the muslin so that the lower edges of the casings line up with the hems. Neatly stitch along both long edges.

3 With right sides together, fold the muslin in half so the casings line up. Stitch the side seams from the bottom edge of the casing to the bottom edge of the bag. Trim the seams and turn right sides out.

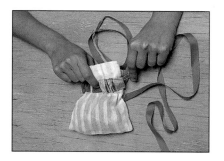

4 Cut the ribbon in half, attach a safety pin to one end of one piece and thread it through both casings so that both ends finish up at the same side. Repeat with the other piece, threading it in the other direction. Fill the bag with herbs and it is ready for immediate use.

TANSY SKIN TONIC

*Tansy leaves smell fairly strong, but this tonic will invigorate the skin,
especially if the bottle is kept in the fridge. Splash on the cool herbal liquid
to start the day. Many other herbal infusions make great tonics for a
variety of skin types. Choose an appropriate mixture from the recipes
below and pour it into a beautiful bottle to make a thoughtful gift.*

MATERIALS

*1 large handful tansy leaves
150 ml (¼ pint/⅔ cup) water
150 ml (¼ pint/⅔ cup) milk
small pan
bottle
cotton wool (surgical cotton)*

VARIATIONS

Make a herbal infusion by boiling
25g (1 oz) (double if fresh) of your
chosen dried herb in 450 ml (¾ pint/
2 cups) water and allowing to cool.
For the following recipes, simply
shake the ingredients together in a
stoppered bottle before storing.

ELDERFLOWER SKIN TONIC
(for dry skin)
*50 ml (2 fl oz/ 3½ tbsp) elderflower
infusion
50 ml (2 fl oz/3½ tbsp) rosewater*

LAVENDER SKIN TONIC
(for oily skin)
*75 ml (3 fl oz/5 tbsp) lavender
infusion
25 ml (1 fl oz/1½ tbsp) witch hazel*

1 Put the leaves, water and milk
in a small pan and bring to the
boil. Simmer for 15 minutes, then
allow to cool in the pan.

2 Strain the tonic into a bottle or
jar. Apply cold to the skin on a
piece of cotton wool (surgical cotton).

ROSEMARY HAIR TONIC

Rosemary is a marvellous and effective hair conditioner, especially for dark hair, and is an excellent substitute for mildly medicated shampoos as it is a natural treatment for dandruff and other related scalp conditions. Used in a rinse once a week, it will really improve the health of the hair and make it shine.

MATERIALS

250 ml (8 fl oz/1 cup) fresh rosemary tips
1.2 litres (2 pints/5 cups) bottled water
saucepan
strainer
funnel
stopper bottle

VARIATION

CHAMOMILE HAIR RINSE
If you are making a hair rinse for someone with fair hair, use chamomile instead of rosemary. This recipe is also very good for children's hair. If a chamomile infusion is left in fair hair it is supposed to lighten the colour, especially when it is dried in the sun.

MATERIALS

250 ml (8 fl oz/1 cup) fresh chamomile flowers
1.2 litres (2 pints/5 cups) bottled water

Make the hair rinse as in method.

1 Put both the ingredients into a saucepan and bring to the boil. Simmer for about 20 minutes, then allow the mixture to cool in the pan.

2 Strain the mixture and pour it into a clean, stoppered bottle. Use as a rinse after shampooing the hair.

PEPPERMINT FOOT-BATH

*This rejuvenating pick-me-up for tired and aching feet will be much appreciated
at the end of a long and active day. The quantities given here make enough to
mix into four foot-baths. To use, fill a large bowl with moderately hot water,
stir in some of the peppermint mixture and soak the feet for 10 minutes.*

MATERIALS

*several stems fresh peppermint
or 65 g (2½ oz/1¼ cups) dried
peppermint leaves
130 g (4½ oz/1⅛ cup) juniper berries
non-aluminium saucepan with lid
750 ml (1¼ pints/3 cups) water
12 drops sandalwood essential oil
6 drops cypress essential oil
coffee filter paper
funnel
storage jars or bottles
labels*

1 Place the fresh or dried peppermint leaves with the juniper
berries in the saucepan and add the
water. Heat slowly to just below
boiling point, stirring occasionally.

2 Remove from the heat, cover the
saucepan and leave to cool.
When the mixture is cold, add the
sandalwood and cypress essential oils
and stir well.

TIP
Choose decorative bottles or jars
and don't forget to include
instructions for using the mixture,
and a list of its contents, when you
label them.

3 Strain off the liquid through a
coffee filter paper in a funnel
into storage jars or bottles. Seal the
containers and label clearly.

HERB-SCENTED SHELLS

If you have brought a pretty collection of seashells back from a summer holiday, here is an easy way to give them an extra dimension. A basket or dish filled with scented shells makes a lovely decoration for the bathroom.

MATERIALS

collection of seashells
dishwashing liquid
bleach
towel
small cuttlefish bone
25 drops lemon essential oil
15 drops bay essential oil
5 drops rosemary essential oil
plastic container with tight-fitting lid
1 vanilla pod (bean)
dish or basket

1 Carefully scrub and wash the shells in a solution of dishwashing liquid and a little bleach, to thoroughly clean them. Set them aside on a towel until they are completely dry.

2 Moisten a cuttlefish bone with the essential oils. Place it in a plastic container with the shells and a bruised vanilla pod (bean). Seal and leave for 4 weeks. Remove the shells and place in a dish or basket.

TIP
These scented shells should last for several weeks, and you can refill the plastic container with shells to repeat the process as often as you wish. Refresh the cuttlefish bone occasionally with a few more drops of essential oils.

SCENTED WOODEN BRUSHES

*Wooden brushes and accessories can be given a delightful fragrance with
a very tiny amount of essential oil. The oil will be absorbed by the bristles
and the wood, and will impart a fragrance for quite some time. Use an
unvarnished hairbrush for this, as it will not be damaged by the oil.*

MATERIALS

*wooden hairbrush, unvarnished
essential oil, such as lavender
wooden hair clip (barette), unvarnished*

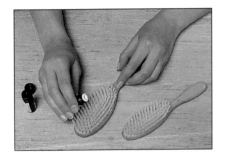

1 Take the wooden hairbrush and
sprinkle two or three drops of
your favourite essential oil on to the
bristle side. Whenever the scent
fades, add a little more oil. As you
brush your hair, a lingering fragrance
will be left on the strands.

2 To add more fragrance to the
hair, sprinkle a couple of drops
of essential oil on to a wooden hair
clip (barette). This too should be
unvarnished. Do not use too much
oil on the clip or the hairbrush as it
will become very messy.

TIP

Once you have introduced this
lovely idea, your friend will want
to continue it, so you could include
a bottle of your chosen essential oil
to complete your gift.

LEMON GRASS, CORIANDER AND CLOVE BATH

*This is a good mixture for anyone suffering from stiff limbs after
excessive exercise. Add it to a bath while the water is running, to help
stimulate the circulation and relieve pain in joints and muscles, as well as
moisturizing the skin. You could make it for an enthusiastic gardener or a
sports-loving friend.*

MATERIALS

spoon
*150 ml (¼ pint/⅔ cup) sweet
almond oil*
small dish
10 drops lemon grass essential oil
10 drops coriander essential oil
10 drops clove essential oil
funnel
stoppered bottle
label

VARIATION

LAVENDER AND MARJORAM BATH
This soothing bath mixture will
relieve the stresses and strains of a
busy day and induce sound sleep.
You could include with this a muslin
bag containing fresh lavender and
marjoram to be added to the water
to enhance the relaxing effect.

MATERIALS

*150 ml (¼ pint/⅔ cup) sweet
almond oil*
35 drops lavender essential oil
15 drops marjoram essential oil

Mix all the ingredients as in method.

1 Carefully spoon the almond oil
into a small dish.

2 Slowly drop in the essential
oils. Mix all the ingredients
together gently and using the funnel,
pour into a bottle. Seal and label.

HERB-FILLED POT-MAT

This aromatic mat, filled with cinnamon, cloves and bay leaves, will protect tabletops from hot pots and pans. The heat immediately releases the piquant aroma of the filling. The mat is made from cotton ticking, perfectly set off by the mattress-style ties which keep the contents evenly distributed.

MATERIALS

*scissors
cotton ticking, 62 x 55 cm
(24½ x 21½ in)
matching sewing thread
needle
iron
pins
dried bay leaves, cloves and
cinnamon sticks to fill
heavy-duty upholstery needle
fine cotton string*

1 To make the hanger, cut a strip of cotton ticking 5 x 30 cm (2 x 12 in). With right sides facing, fold in half lengthways. Stitch the long side, leaving the ends open. Trim the seam. Turn right side out and press. Fold in half to form a loop. Cut two rectangles of fabric measuring 31 x 50 cm (12¼ x 20 in).

2 Place the two pieces right sides together, then slip the hanging loop between the layers, with the raw edges pointing out towards one corner. Pin and stitch the pieces together, leaving a 7.5 cm (3 in) gap open in one side. Trim the seams. Turn the mat right side out.

3 Fill the cushion loosely with the herbs and spices. Slip stitch the opening securely.

4 Using a heavy-duty upholstery needle threaded with fine cotton string, make a stitch through both layers about one-third of the way in from two sides of the mat. Clear the filling away from the area as you go. Knot the string, and trim and fray the ends. Make three more ties in the same way.

PATCHWORK HERB SACHET

The patchwork star worked on this herb-filled sachet is based on the eight-point Lone Star motif which appears on many early American quilts.

MATERIALS

pencil
tracing paper
thin card (cardboard) for templates
scissors
thick paper
ruler
fabric marker
mustard yellow cotton fabric,
12.5 x 20 cm (5 x 8 in)
green-and-white check cotton fabric,
12.5 x 20 cm (5 x 8 in)
dark orange cotton fabric, 20 x 40 cm
(8 x 16 in)
backing paper
tacking (basting) thread
needle
matching sewing thread
iron
pins
dried herbs or pot-pourri to fill
small pearl button

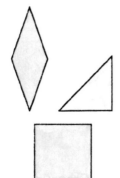

1 Enlarge the templates and transfer to card (cardboard). Cut eight diamonds, four squares and four triangles from the paper. Draw on to the fabric, following the grain and adding 5 mm (¼ in) all around.

2 Cut out four yellow and four check diamonds, four orange squares and four orange triangles. Lay a backing paper on each shape, turn the seam allowances over the paper, and tack (baste) in place.

3 Overstitch a yellow and a check diamond together along one edge. Sew an orange square into the right angle. Make four of these units, then join together to form a star. Sew the orange triangles into the remaining spaces. Press and remove the tacking (basting) threads.

4 Cut a 19 cm (7½ in) square from orange fabric. Press under 5 mm (¼ in) all around. With wrong sides together, pin to the patchwork and overstitch the outside edge leaving a 7.5 cm (3 in) gap. Fill with herbs or pot-pourri and sew up. Sew a small pearl button to the centre.

PRESSED HERB CARDS

A home-made card will invariably be treasured long after the celebration is over.
Although it takes time and trouble to make your own cards, you could spend a
free evening making a batch, then keep them for suitable occasions. Cover your
design with the clear self-adhesive film made for covering books.

MATERIALS

pressed herbs and flowers, such as
blue cornflower, ivy, rosemary, borage
blank greetings card
tweezers
large tapestry needle
PVA (white) glue
clear self-adhesive plastic film

1 Arrange a selection of pressed herbs and flowers on the front of the card. They can be laid randomly or in a pattern. Use tweezers to position the pieces.

2 When the design is complete, use a large tapestry needle to slide small dabs of glue under the flowers without moving them. Cover the design with clear film.

TIP
Buy small diaries or address books and decorate the front covers with pressed leaves and flowers. Use tweezers to arrange the flowers in a pattern, fix in place with glue and cover with clear film as described in method.

ROSE AND LAVENDER SCENTED CUSHION

Fragrant cushions are a charming way to scent a room, releasing a subtle
perfume every time someone leans against them. The fragrance will last well,
but make the cushion cover removable so that the mixture can be replaced
when it has lost its freshness.

MATERIALS

50 g (2 oz) dried rose petals and buds
10 g (¼ oz) dried lavender flowers
10 g (¼ oz) dried oakmoss (optional)
5 bay leaves, crumbled
15 ml (1 tbsp) ground cinnamon
15 ml (1 tbsp) ground orris root
10 drops rose essential oil
muslin, 40 cm (16 in) square
matching sewing thread
needle
thick polyester wadding (batting),
50 cm (20 in) square
cushion cover, 25 cm (10 in) square

1 Mix all the dry ingredients in a bowl and add the rose essential oil. The ground orris root will act as a fixative for the other fragrances and make them last longer.

2 Fold the muslin in four and stitch seams along two sides to create a bag 20 cm (8 in) square. Fill with the aromatic mixture and stitch the opening closed.

3 Place the scented bag on the thick polyester wadding (batting) and fold it over the bag. Stitch around the wadding to create a square pad for the cushion. Slip the scented cushion pad into the cover.

SCENTED SACHETS

Scented sachets and bags are welcome in any home: they can be used to scent drawers and cupboards, tucked in amongst the sofa cushions or put under the pillow to encourage sweet dreams. The most traditional of all sweet bags is the lavender bag, which has always been popular because it is not only deliciously fragrant, but also keeps clothes moths at bay.

MATERIALS

(to make five bags)
scissors
fabric, 30 x 120 cm (12 x 48 in)
matching sewing thread
needle
pins
iron
75 g (3 oz/1 cup) lavender or other
scented flowers or leaves
25 g (1 oz/2 tbsp) ground orris root
25 drops lavender or other essential oil
1.25 m (1½ yd) ribbon or cord
(optional)

1 Cut the fabric lengthways into two pieces, making one piece 25 x 120 cm (10 x 48 in) and the other 5 x 120 cm (2 x 48 in). Cut each piece of fabric into five equal pieces. The larger pieces will make the bags and the smaller pieces will make the ties. Turn in a 5 cm (2 in) seam allowance along one edge of each bag and hem.

2 Fold each bag in half, right sides together, and pin along the unhemmed edges. Stitch along the pin line. Turn the right way out and press. To make the ties, fold the smaller pieces of fabric in half lengthways, pin and stitch along the side and across one end. Turn the right way out. Fold in and stitch the unfinished end, then press.

3 Divide the filling equally between the bags and fasten each one with a tie. Alternatively, you can fasten each bag with a 25 cm (10 in) piece of ribbon or cord.

INDEX

Publisher's Acknowledgements

The publishers would like to thank the
following people for designing and
making the projects in this book:
Fiona Barnett, Penny Boylan, Andi
Clevely, Stephanie Donaldson, Roger
Egerickx, Tessa Evelegh, Terence Moore,
Katherine Richmond, Sally Walton

Photographers
James Duncan, John Freeman, Michelle
Garrett, Debbie Patterson